Bond

UP TO *SPEED* English
Tests and Papers

10–11+ years

Sarah Lindsay

Text © Sarah Lindsay 2013

The right of Sarah Lindsay to be identified as author of this work has been asserted by her in accordance with the Copyright, Designs and Patents Act 1988.

All rights reserved. No part of this publication may be reproduced or transmitted in any form or by any means, electronic or mechanical, including photocopy, recording or any information storage and retrieval system, without permission in writing from the publisher or under licence from the Copyright Licensing Agency Limited, of Saffron House, 6–10 Kirby Street, London, EC1N 8TS.

Any person who commits any unauthorised act in relation to this publication may be liable to criminal prosecution and civil claims for damages.

Published in 2013 by:
Nelson Thornes Ltd
Delta Place
27 Bath Road
CHELTENHAM
GL53 7TH
United Kingdom

13 14 15 16 17 / 10 9 8 7 6 5 4 3 2 1

A catalogue record for this book is available from the British Library

ISBN 978 1 4085 1887 8

Page make-up by OKS Prepress, India

Printed in China by 1010 Printing International Ltd

Acknowledgements

The author and the publisher would like to thank the following for permission to reproduce material:

P12 'Aliens Stole My Underpants' by Brian Moses from *Behind the Staffroom Door: The Very Best of Brian Moses*, published by Macmillan (2007); p22 'The Great Mouse Plot' by Roald Dahl from *Boy – Tales of Childhood*, published by Jonathan Cape, an imprint of Penguin Books Ltd; p32 from *Victory* by Susan Cooper, published by Corgi Books (2007). Reproduced by permission of Random House Children's Books; p39 'The Apple Raid' by Vernon Scannell from *The Apple Raid*, published by Chatto & Windus (1974). Reproduced by kind permission of the author's estate; pp44–45 from *Stuff that scares your pants off!* by Glen Murphy, published by Macmillan Children's Books (2009); p50 'One Spared to the Sea' from *The Hogboon of Hell* by Nancy and W. Towrie Cutt, published by Andre Deutsch (1979).

Every effort has been made to trace the copyright holders but if any have been inadvertently overlooked the publisher will be pleased to make the necessary arrangements at the first opportunity.

Introduction

What is Bond?

The Bond *Up to Speed* series is a new addition to the Bond range of assessment papers, the number one series for the 11+, selective exams and general practice. Bond *Up to Speed* is carefully designed to support children who need less challenging activities than those in the regular age-appropriate Bond papers, in order to build up and improve their techniques and confidence.

How does this book work?

The book contains two distinct sets of papers, along with full answers and a Progress Chart:

- Focus tests, accompanied by advice and directions, are focused on particular (and age-appropriate) English question types encountered in the 11+ and other exams. The questions are deliberately set at a less challenging level than the standard *Assessment Papers*. Each Focus test is designed to help a child 'catch' their level in a particular question type, and then gently raise it through the course of the test and the subsequent Mixed papers.

- Mixed papers are longer tests containing a full range of English question types. These are designed to provide rigorous practice with less-challenging questions, perhaps against the clock, in order to help children acquire and develop the necessary skills and techniques for 11+ success.

Full answers are provided for both types of test in the middle of the book.

How much time should the tests take?

The tests are for practice and to reinforce learning, and you may wish to test exam techniques and working to a set time limit. Using the Mixed papers, we would recommend that your child spends 50 minutes answering the 80 questions in each paper, plus 5 minutes for reading the comprehension extract.

You can reduce the suggested time by 5 minutes to practise working at speed.

Using the Progress Chart

The Progress Chart can be used to track Focus test and Mixed paper results over time to monitor how well your child is doing and identify any repeated problems in tackling the different question types.

Focus test 1 Spelling 1

Add the missing double letters to each of these words.

> It is always important to recognise words that use double letters.

1 a ____ ____ empt

2 co ____ ____ ittee

3 discu ____ ____ ion

4 a ____ ____ ention

5 gra ____ ____ ar

6 di ____ ____ erent

6

Each of these words has a silent letter. Circle the silent letter in each word.

> Say the word out loud to help you hear which letter is silent.

7 island   8 knight

9 scenery   10 design

11 crumb   12 budget

6

Write the **plural** form of each of these **nouns**.

> Remember, for most words ending in a consonant and y, you drop the y and add ies.

13 lady   _____

14 country   _____

15 toy   _____

16 baby   _____

17 trolley   _____

18 fly   _____

6

Write each of these words correctly.

> **Clue: think of the spelling rules.**

19 queit _quiet_

20 sleepyly _sleeply_

21 jiant _giant_

22 churchs _churches_

23 carefull _careful_

24 resipe _resipie_

6

Add a **prefix** to each of these words to make a new word.

> **A prefix is added to the beginning of a word to change its meaning.**

un   im   il

25 _un_ broken un

26 _____ polite un

27 _un_ pure im

28 _____ legal il

29 _un_ founded un

30 _il_ logical il

6

Now go to the Progress Chart to record your score!   Total   **30**

5

Focus test 2 — Sentences 1

What are the following: commands, questions or statements?

> **Clue: what end punctuation mark would you use?**

1 Shall we call at Georgia's house _____
2 Why do I have to go to bed early _____
3 Don't run _____
4 It is nearly time for tea _____
5 My ear is really sore _____
6 Stop arguing with your brother _____

6

Underline the letters in this passage that should be capitals.

> **Capital letters are used at the beginning of sentences and for proper nouns.**

7–13 as emily ran towards cirencester park, she knew she was late. she just hoped archie had waited for her. he was going to swap his movie with her *harry potter* book but she knew he would be in a hurry.

7

Improve each of these sentences by adding a **clause** or **phrase**.

> **A clause is a section of a sentence with a verb, a phrase is a group of words that act as a unit.**

14 Mr Churchill kept an eye on the children in the pool.

Mr charch _____

_____

15 The ponies roamed free on the moor.

_____

_____

16 The lioness showed her cubs the food.

_____

_____

17 The car made a quick getaway.

_____

_____

18 Jess watched a film.

_____

_____　⟨5⟩

Change the word in bold into the **past tense**.

> If something is written in the past tense, it means it has already happened.

19 George **sleeps** in front of the television. _____ slept _____

20 Jacob **finds** his homework tricky. _____ found _____

21 Aimee **rides** every week until the holiday. _____ rode _____

22 On Monday Aaron **goes** to judo. _____ went _____

23 The dishwasher **makes** a funny sound. _____ made _____

24 The rain **pours** throughout the night. _____ pour. _____　⟨6⟩

Punctuate this sentence correctly.

> Don't forget speech marks, commas, full stops and so on.

25–30 When will tea be ready moaned Freddie I'm starving It has to be soon

"when will the tea be ready" moaned Fredy i'm starving
it has to be soon.　⟨6⟩

Now go to the Progress Chart to record your score! Total ⟨30⟩

Focus test 3 | Grammar 1

Write two examples of each of the following.

> Proper noun – the name of a person or place and so on
> Abstract noun – a word referring to a concept or idea
> Collective noun – a word referring to a group

1–2 proper noun   _____   _____

3–4 abstract noun   _____   _____

5–6 collective noun   _____   _____   **6**

Form **verbs** from each of the following.

> These words are nouns, for example: the noun *production* gives the
> verb *produce*.

7 discussion   _____

8 division   _____

9 alteration   _____

10 dictation   _____

11 creation   _____

12 celebration   _____   **6**

Write two **adjectives** to describe each of these **nouns**.

> An adjective describes someone or something.

13 _____, _____ pond

14 _____, _____ cloud

15 _____, _____ throne

16 _____, _____ woman

17 _____, _____ bone

18 _____, _____ sportsman   **6**

8

Add a different **conjunction** to each of these sentences.

> Conjunctions are sometimes referred to as connectives. They are words that join together words, phrases or clauses.

19 The dog raced towards the pond _____ he got covered in mud!

20 Dan phoned Harry _____ he needed to ask him something.

21 The neighbours were irritating _____ they played their music too loud.

22 Ben finished his homework carefully _____ he could go out to play.

23 Megan ate her tea quickly _____ it gave her hiccups.

24 Jake laughed _____ he hadn't understood the joke.

6

Underline the **preposition** in each sentence.

> A preposition relates words to each other.

25 The squirrel jumped towards the branch.

26 Hannah found her homework in the dog bed!

27 The mouse hid behind the pot plant.

28 Ben put his drink inside his bag.

29 I climbed over the fallen tree.

30 The pigeon sat alone on the telephone wire.

6

Now go to the Progress Chart to record your score!   Total   30

Focus test 4 | Vocabulary 1

Write an **abbreviation** for each of these.

> An abbreviation is a word or words that are shortened.

1 Doctor　　　　　_____

2 United States　　_____

3 centimetre　　　_____

4 Limited　　　　　_____

5 hour　　　　　　_____

6 Great Britain　　_____

6

Put these words in **alphabetical order**.

> Alphabetical order is the order you would find words in a dictionary.

nun　　nuzzle　　nutmeg　　number　　nurse　　nutty

7 _____　　　8 _____

9 _____　　10 _____

11 _____　　12 _____

6

Write a **metaphor** for each of these subjects.

> A metaphor is an expression in which something is described in terms usually associated with something else, for example: 'the blanket of snow lay on the ground'.

13 a thick frost

_____

14 a duvet

_____

15 thunder

_____

16 a burning fire

_____

17 autumn leaves

_____

⬤ 5

Underline the **root words** in each of these words.

> A root word is the word to which prefixes and suffixes are added to make another word.

18 unclean

19 agreeable

20 destructive

21 impure

22 inspection

23 planning

⬤ 6

Using a word from each column, write seven **compound words**.

> A compound word is a word made up of two words, for example toothbrush.

24 night   dog

25 arm   due

26 bull   gown

27 chop   hole

28 day   chair

29 key   stick

30 over   dream

⬤ 7

Now go to the Progress Chart to record your score!   Total ⬤ 30

Focus test 5 Comprehension 1

Aliens Stole My Underpants

To understand the ways
of alien beings is hard,
and I've never worked it out
why they landed in my backyard.

And I've always wondered why 5
on their journey to the stars,
these aliens stole my underpants
and took them back to Mars.

They came on a Monday night
when the weekend wash had been done, 10
pegged out on the line
to be dried by the morning sun.

Mrs Driver from next door
was a witness at the scene
when aliens snatched my underpants – 15
I'm glad that they were clean!

It seems they were quite choosy
as nothing else was taken.
Do aliens wear underpants
or were they just mistaken? 20

I think I have a theory
as to what they wanted them for,
they needed to block off a draught
blowing in through the spacecraft door.

Or maybe some Mars museum 25
wanted items brought back from space.
Just think of my pair of Y-fronts
displayed in their own glass case.

And on the label beneath
would be written where they got 'em 30
and how such funny underwear
once covered an Earthling's bottom!

Brian Moses

Answer these questions.

1   Where did the aliens land?

_____

2   Where were the aliens believed to be heading?

_____

3   Which day of the week did the aliens arrive?

_____

4   Where did the aliens come from?

_____

5–6   Write two pieces of evidence that suggest the aliens removed the underpants.

_____

_____

7   What is meant by line 17 'It seems they were quite choosy'?

_____

8–9   What two reasons were given for why the underpants went missing?

_____

_____

10   How do we know that this poem is written from a boy's perspective?

_____

11   What is an 'Earthling' (line 32)

_____

12–13   Is this a rhyming poem? Give a reason for your answer.

_____

_____

14–15   Which verse do you most enjoy? Why?

_____

_____

_____

Now go to the Progress Chart to record your score!   Total   15

Focus test 6 — Spelling 2

Circle the word that is spelled correctly.

These are tricky words. You may need a dictionary to help!

1	necessary	necessery
2	embarassed	embarrassed
3	similar	simular
4	temprature	temperature
5	separate	seperate
6	occasional	occassional

6

Add *ance* or *ence* to each of these to make a word.

7 refer_____

8 obedi_____

9 extravag_____

10 lic_____

11 ignor_____

12 fragr_____

6

Circle the unstressed vowel in each of these words.

An unstressed vowel is a vowel within a word that is hard to hear.

13 general

14 secretary

15 interest

16 dictionary

17 original

18 family

6

14

Add *ie* or *ei* to each of these to make a word.

> Remember '*i* before *e* except after *c*, or when the word sound is not *ee*'

19 rev _____ _____ w   20 v _____ _____ l

21 th _____ _____ r   22 f _____ _____ rce

23 f _____ _____ ry   24 c _____ _____ ling

6

Write the **contraction** for each of these pairs of words.

> A contraction is when two words are shortened into one.

25 they + will   = _____

26 I + have   = _____

27 he + will   = _____

28 is + not   = _____

29 should + have   = _____

30 there + is   = _____

6

Now go to the Progress Chart to record your score!   Total   30

15

Focus test 7 Sentences 2

Add the missing commas to these sentences.

> *Commas are needed when there is a slight pause in the sentence or to separate items in a list.*

1 To make ice cubes pour cold water into the mould and put in the freezer.

2–3 The old lady frail and unsteady carried her shopping home.

4 Carys collected her certificate medal and winning prize money from the major.

5–6 The mango sweet and juicy tasted delicious.

6

Rewrite these sentences, changing them from **plural** to **singular**.

> *When you have changed the nouns to their singular form, reread the sentence to check that it still all makes sense.*

7 The farmers are concerned about the crops.

_____

8 The children were excited on the last day of term.

_____

9 The strawberries tasted delicious.

_____

10 The firemen bravely put out the fire in the flats.

_____

11 The windows were left open and the people were cold.

5

_____

16

Draw a line (/) every time a new line should have started in the following dialogue.

> A new line should be started every time a new person starts to speak.

12–17 "I can't wait for the performance," said Ellie. "Nor can I!" replied Dan. "Which scene are you in?" asked Tuhil. "I'm in the first scene," said Dan. "I bet I feel very nervous the first time we do it." "I know I will be terrified but I still can't wait," laughed Izzy. "Shall we practise at playtime?" Ellie asked. "Great idea!" they all responded.

6

Rewrite these sentences, adding the missing punctuation and capital letters.

> Always check through your work carefully to make sure that you have picked up all the missing punctuation and capital letters.

18–22 please can i take your dog for a walk asked julia

_____

_____

23–30 i am so tired said simon yawning i am going to bed early tonight

_____

_____

13

Now go to the Progress Chart to record your score! Total 30

17

Focus test 8 · Grammar 2

Write three sentences, each including an **adjective** and a **verb**.

> An adjective describes someone or something. A verb is a doing or being word.

1–2 _____

3–4 _____

5–6 _____ **6**

Circle the **pronouns**.

> A pronoun is a word usually used to replace a noun.

7–12
up	mine	his
soon	under	you
they	because	theirs
know	see	I

6

Choose the **adverb** that would best describe each **verb**.

> An adverb provides information about place (for example, here), time (for example, soon) or manner (for example, quickly).

often	carefully	slowly
soon	speedily	playfully

13 The sprinter ran _____ .

14 I'm sure your grandparents will _____ arrive.

15 The cat _____ moved towards the mouse.

16 As the children _____ splashed in the pool, their mother looked on.

17 Niall _____ ate his breakfast.

18 Molly _____ sat and read.

6

In each of these sentences a word is incorrect. Underline the word and rewrite it correctly.

Look carefully at the verbs!

19 The twins tried to caught the ball. _____

20 We think you would liked to go. _____

21 It were time to leave. _____

22 Jay had to ate his breakfast quickly. _____

23 Freya write a letter to her penfriend. _____

24 Elliot find a Roman coin. _____ 6

Circle the word that is:

25	a verb	him	cake	going	up
26	an adjective	cloudy	jump	from	it
27	an adverb	leotard	there	was	party
28	a noun	several	his	choir	near
29	a preposition	shaded	love	me	beneath
30	a verb	now	ate	happily	onto

6

Now go to the Progress Chart to record your score! Total 30

Focus test 9 · Vocabulary 2

Write six **synonyms** for the word 'see'.

> A synonym is a word with the same or similar meaning to another word.

1–6 _____ _____ _____

_____ _____ _____

6

Write two **onomatopoeic** words that describe the sound this thing makes.

> Onomatopoeic words echo a sound associated with its meaning.

7–8 a cat _____ _____

9–10 a bird _____ _____

11–12 a car _____ _____

6

Write a **definition** for each of these words.

> A definition is the meaning of a word.
> Use a dictionary to help if you are stuck on a word.

13 playground

_____

14 safari

_____

15 invisible

_____

16 drowsy

_____

17 soundproof

_____

18 verdict

_____

6

Circle the **diminutives**.

> A diminutive is a word implying smallness.

19–24

goose	droplet	minibus	flute
kitchenette	fly	piglet	duckling
hour	miniskirt	cup	key

6

Write 'there', 'their' or 'they're' in each gap. Don't forget capital letters if necessary.

> There, their and there are homophones. Homophones are words that have the same sound as another word but a different meaning or spelling.

25 _____ are my trainers, I wondered where they were!

26–27 _____ going to buy some with _____ money.

28 Is it _____ turn or mine?

29 Do you think _____ going to be late?

30 Do we need to go _____ tonight?

6

Now go to the Progress Chart to record your score!   Total   30

Focus test 10   Comprehension 2

The Great Mouse Plot

My four friends and I had come across a loose floor-board at the back of the classroom, and when we prised it up with a blade of a pocket-knife, we discovered a big hollow space underneath. This, we decided, would be our secret hiding place for sweets and other small treasures such as conkers and monkey-nuts and birds' eggs. Every afternoon, when the last lesson was over, the five of us would wait until the classroom had emptied, then we would lift up the floor-board and examine our secret hoard, perhaps adding to it or taking something away.   5

One day, when we lifted it up, we found a dead mouse lying among our treasures. It was an exciting discovery. Thwaites took it out by its tail and waved it in front of our faces. 'What shall we do with it?' he cried.   10

'It stinks!' someone shouted. 'Throw it out of the window quick!'

'Hold on a tick,' I said. 'Don't throw it away.'

Thwaites hesitated. They all looked at me.

When writing about oneself, one must strive to be truthful. Truth is more important than modesty. I must tell you, therefore, that it was I and I alone who had the idea for the great   15 and daring Mouse Plot. We all have our moments of brilliance and glory, and this was mine.

'Why don't we,' I said, 'slip it into one of Mrs Pratchett's jars of sweets? Then when she puts her dirty hand in to grab a handful, she'll grab a stinky dead mouse instead.'

The other four stared at me in wonder. Then, as the sheer genius of the plot began to sink in, they all started grinning. They slapped me on the back. They cheered me and   20 danced around the classroom. 'We'll do it today!' they cried. 'We'll do it on the way home! *You* had the idea,' they said to me, 'so *you* can be the one to put the mouse in the jar.'

Thwaites handed me the mouse. I put it into my trouser pocket. Then the five of us left the school, crossed the village green and headed for the sweet-shop. We were tremendously jazzed up. We felt like a gang of desperados setting out to rob a train or blow up the sheriff's office.   25

'Make sure you put it into a jar which is used often,' somebody said.

'I'm putting it in Gobstoppers,' I said. 'The Gobstopper jar is never behind the counter.'

'I've got a penny,' Thwaites said, 'so I'll ask for one Sherbert Sucker and one Bootlace. And while she turns away to get them, you slip the mouse in quickly with the Gobstoppers.'

Thus everything was arranged. We were strutting a little as we entered the shop. We   30 were the victors now and Mrs Pratchett was the victim. She stood behind the counter, and her small malignant pig-eyes watched us suspiciously as we came forward.

'One Sherbet Sucker, please,' Thwaites said to her, holding out his penny.

I kept to the rear of the group, and when I saw Mrs Pratchett turn her head away for a couple of seconds to fish a Sherbert Sucker out of the box, I lifted the heavy glass lid   35 of the Gobstopper jar and dropped the mouse in. Then I replaced the lid as silently as possible. My heart was thumping like mad and my hands had gone all sweaty.

'And one Bootlace, please,' I heard Thwaites saying. When I turned round, I saw Mrs Pratchett holding out the Bootlace in her filthy fingers.

'I don't want all the lot of you troopin' in 'ere if only one of you is buyin',' she screamed   40 at us. 'Now beat it! Go on, get out!'

As soon as we were outside, we broke into a run. 'Did you do it?' they shouted at me.

'Of course I did!' I said.

'Well done you!' they cried. 'What a super show!'

I felt like a hero. I *was* a hero. It was marvellous to be so popular.   45

From *Boy*, Roald Dahl's autobiography

22

Answer these questions.

1 Where was the secret hiding place?

2 What was hidden in the secret hiding place?

3 Why do you think the friends were excited about finding a dead mouse?

4 Whose idea was it to do something with the mouse?

5 What is Roald Dahl suggesting when he says, 'We all have our moments of brilliance and glory, and this was mine.'

6 What do the friends plan to do with the mouse?

7 Does the passage suggest that the sweet shop is far from the school?

8–9 Describe how you think Roald Dahl felt as he approached the shop.

10 Was Roald Dahl successful in executing the plan?

11 Which line in the passage suggests how nervous Roald Dahl was?

12–13 The friends obviously don't like Mrs Pratchett very much. Find two pieces of evidence in the passage that support this.

14–15 How do you think Mrs Pratchett would have felt on discovering the mouse. Explain your answer.

Now go to the Progress Chart to record your score!   Total   15

Focus test 11 — Spelling 3

Each of these words has a missing silent letter. Rewrite each word correctly.

1 sience _____

2 nome _____

3 sissors _____

4 thum _____

5 autum _____

6 onest _____

> Silent letters can be at the beginning, middle or end of the word.

6

Match these **prefixes** with their meanings.

> Think of a word with the prefix. This may help give you a clue to its meaning.

7 aqua across

8 aero against

9 trans distance/from afar

10 micro water

11 tele air

12 anti small

6

Write the **plural** form of each of these **nouns**.

> Remember, for most words ending in an *f* or *fe*, you drop the *f* or *fe* and add *ves*.

13 thief _____

14 knife _____

15 calf _____

16 elf _____

17 half _____

18 wife _____

6

Add the **suffixes** to these words ending in *y*.

> Don't forget any necessary spelling changes.

19 easy + ly = _____

20 carry + er = _____

21 journey + ing = _____

22 play + ful = _____

23 busy + est = _____

24 employ + ment = _____

6

Write each of these words correctly.

> Each word has a missing letter.

25 akward _____

26 boundry _____

27 defnite _____

28 encourge _____

29 haras _____

30 interupt _____

6

Now go to the Progress Chart to record your score! Total 30

Focus test 12   Sentences 3

State whether each of these sentences has an **active** or **passive verb**.

> An *active verb* is when the main person or thing *does* the action.
> A *passive verb* is when the main person or thing has the action *done to it*.

1   Daniel kicked the ball.   _____

2   Dad had a drink spilled over him.   _____

3   Nazar swam six lengths of the pool.   _____

4   Tisha was hit by the frisbee.   _____

5   Inky, the dog, was given a bath.   _____

6   Jane finished her homework.   _____

6

Change the following sentences into **reported speech**.

> Reported speech states what has been said without using the
> exact words or speech marks.

7   "It is time for tea," said Mum.

_____

8   "When do the holidays start?" asked Joe.

_____

9   "Do I have to clean out my rabbit?" Jacob queried.

_____

10   "I am off to the park now," said Mia.

_____

11   "I think the phone is ringing," stated Tom.

_____

5

Rewrite these sentences without the double negatives.

> Double negatives within a sentence don't actually make sense!

12   I don't want no sympathy.

_____

26

13 Please can I not have no cheese in my sandwich.

_____

14 I can't find no biscuits!

_____

15 Anika won't catch no bus home.

_____

16 There isn't no fruit growing on the trees.

_____   5

Rewrite each of the following, using only two words, one of which should have an apostrophe.

> An apostrophe shows when something belongs to someone or something. For example, whiskers belonging to a lion = lion's whiskers.

17 lead belonging to the dog   _____

18 coat belonging to Callum   _____

19 pen belonging to teacher   _____

20 hat belonging to policeman   _____

21 radio belonging to the painter _____

22 cake belonging to the girl   _____   6

Rewrite this sentence, adding the missing punctuation and capital letters.

> Remember, always check through your work carefully.

23–30 are you awake Toby whispered it is time for our midnight feast

_____

_____   8

Now go to the Progress Chart to record your score!   Total   30

27

Focus test 13 — Grammar 3

Complete the table.

> Comparative adjectives compare two nouns, superlative adjectives compare more than two nouns. Note: not all words need a suffix added.

1–6

	Comparative adjectives	Superlative adjectives
tall		
tired		most tired
good	better	
attractive		

6

What parts of speech are each of these words?

> Each of the following parts of speech will match with one word below.

common noun   proper noun   collective noun   abstract noun

adjective   verb   adverb   connective

preposition   pronoun

7 inside   _____

8 Kyle   _____

9 bat   _____

10 so   _____

11 heartily   _____

12 flock   _____

13 they   _____

14 happiness   _____

15 thought   _____

16 miserable   _____

10

28

Answers will vary for questions that require the child to answer in their own words. Possible answers to most of these questions are given in *italics*.

Focus test 1: Spelling 1

1	attempt	2	committee
3	discussion	4	attention
5	grammar	6	different
7	s	8	k
9	c	10	g
11	b	12	d
13	ladies	14	countries
15	toys	16	babies
17	trolleys	18	flies
19	quiet/quite	20	sleepily
21	giant	22	churches
23	careful	24	recipe
25	unbroken	26	impolite
27	impure	28	illegal
29	unfounded	30	illogical

Focus test 2: Sentences 1

1	question	2	question
3	command	4	statement
5	statement	6	command

7–13 **A**s **E**mily ran towards **C**irencester **P**ark, she knew she was late. **S**he just hoped **A**rchie had waited for her. **H**e was going to swap his movie with her *Harry Potter* book but she knew he would be in a hurry.

14–18 *Sentences improved with the addition of a phrase or clause, e.g. Mr Churchill kept an eye on the children in the pool as they dived in the deep end to retrieve their goggles.*

19	slept	20	found
21	rode	22	went
23	made	24	poured

25–30 "When will tea be ready?" moaned Freddie. "I'm starving! It has to be soon."

Focus test 3: Grammar 1

1–2 *Tim, India*
3–4 *love, hate*
5–6 *swarm, herd*
7 discuss

8 divide
9 alter
10 dictate
11 create
12 celebrate

13–18 *Adjectives describing the given nouns, for example dark, murky pond.*

19 *and*
20 *as*
21 *because*
22 *so*
23 *but*
24 *although*
25 towards
26 in
27 behind
28 inside
29 over
30 on

Focus test 4: Vocabulary 1

1	Dr	2	US
3	cm	4	Ltd
5	hr	6	GB
7	number	8	nun
9	nurse	10	nutmeg
11	nutty	12	nuzzle

13–17 *Child's own metaphors describing the given subject. A metaphor is a figurative expression in which something is described in terms usually associated with another, for example the sky is a sapphire sea.*

18	clean	19	agree
20	destruct	21	pure
22	inspect	23	plan
24	nightgown	25	armchair
26	bulldog	27	chopstick
28	daydream	29	keyhole
30	overdue		

Focus test 5: Comprehension 1

1 The aliens landed in the backyard.
2 The aliens were believed to be heading for the stars.
3 The aliens arrived on a Monday.
4 The aliens came from Mars.

ANSWERS

Bond UP TO SPEED English Tests and Papers 10–11+ years

A1

ANSWERS

5–6 1 – The underpants had disappeared.
2 – Mrs Driver from next door was a witness.

7 This suggests that the aliens knew what they wanted.

8–9 1 – They were needed to block off a draught.
2 – They were to be displayed in a museum.

10 We know this was written from a boy's perspective as it states the underpants that went missing were 'Y-fronts', underpants that boys wear.

11 An 'Earthling' is someone who lives on Earth.

12–13 Yes, this poem does rhyme. In each verse the 2nd and 4th lines rhyme.

14–15 *Child's favourite verse and why they chose it, for example it made them laugh, it was a clever idea.*

Focus test 6: Spelling 2

1	necessary	**2**	embarrassed
3	similar	**4**	temperature
5	separate	**6**	occasional
7	reference	**8**	obedience
9	extravagance	**10**	licence
11	ignorance	**12**	fragrance
13	a	**14**	a
15	first e	**16**	a
17	a	**18**	i
19	review	**20**	veil
21	their	**22**	fierce
23	fiery	**24**	ceiling
25	they'll	**26**	I've
27	he'll	**28**	isn't
29	should've	**30**	there's

Focus test 7: Sentences 2

1 To make ice cubes, pour cold water into the mould and put in the freezer.

2–3 The old lady, frail and unsteady, carried her shopping home.

4 Carys collected her certificate, medal and winning prize money from the major.

5–6 The mango, sweet and juicy, tasted delicious.

7 The farmer is concerned about the crop.

8 The child was excited on the last day of term.

9 The strawberry tasted delicious.

10 The fireman bravely put out the fire in the flat.

11 The window was left open and the person was cold.

12–17 "I can't wait for the performance," said Ellie. /"Nor can I!" replied Dan. /"Which scene are you in?" asked Tuhil. /"I'm in the first scene," said Dan. "I bet I feel very nervous the first time we do it." /"I know I will be terrified but I still can't wait," laughed Izzy. /"Shall we practise at playtime?" Ellie asked. /"Great idea!" they all responded.

18–22 "**P**lease can I take your dog for a walk**?**" asked **J**ulia.

23–30 "**I** am so tired," said **S**imon yawning. "I am going to bed early tonight."

Focus test 8: Grammar 2

1–6 *Three sentences, each with an adjective and verb.*

7–12 mine, his, you, they, theirs, I

13 speedily

14 soon

15 carefully/slowly/playfully

16 playfully

17 carefully/slowly/speedily

18 often

19 catch

20 like

21 was/is

22 eat

23 wrote

24 found

25 going

26 cloudy

27 there

28 choir

29 beneath

30 ate

Focus test 9: Vocabulary 2

1–6 *observe, glance, peer, inspect, look, stare*

7–8 *miaow, purr*

9–10 *cheep, chirp*

11–12 *beep, vroom*

13 *an area for children to play in*

14 *an expedition to observe or hunt wild animals*

Bond UP TO SPEED English Tests and Papers 10–11+ years

A2

15 *something that can't be seen*
16 *feeling sleepy*
17 *a contained area that doesn't let sound in or out*
18 *a decision of guilt or innocence (or it can be an opinion on something)*
19–24 droplet, minibus, kitchenette, piglet, duckling, miniskirt
25 There
26–27 They're, their
28 their
29 they're
30 there

Focus test 10: Comprehension 2

1 The secret hiding place was under a floorboard at the back of the classroom.
2 Sweets, conkers, monkey-nuts and birds' eggs (treasures) were hidden in the secret hiding place.
3 *Child's own answer suggesting the friends were excited to see the dead mouse as it was something different and unexpected.*
4 It was Roald Dahl's idea to do something with the mouse.
5 Roald Dahl is stating how amazing he is because he had such a wonderful idea!
6 The friends plan to place the dead mouse in a sweet jar to shock Mrs Pratchett.
7 No, the description of how to get to the sweet shop from the school doesn't suggest it is very far – just across the village green.
8–9 Roald Dahl felt excited and daring as he headed for the sweet shop, though he might also have felt nervous.
10 Yes, Roald Dahl successfully placed the mouse in the gobstopper jar.
11 The line 'My heart was thumping like mad and my hands had gone all sweaty.' (line 37) suggests that Roald Dahl was very nervous.
12–13 The friends may not have like Mrs Pratchett because she isn't nice and shouts at them: 'Now beat it! Go on, get out!' (line 41). Also, she always has dirty hands when handling their sweets: 'when she puts her dirty hand in to grab a handful' (lines 17–18).

14–15 *Child's answer empathising with Mrs Pratchett, for example, the shock and horror at what she had discovered.*

Focus test 11: Spelling 3

1	science	2	gnome
3	scissors	4	thumb
5	autumn	6	honest
7	water	8	air
9	across	10	small
11	distance/from afar	12	against
13	thieves	14	knives
15	calves	16	elves
17	halves	18	wives
19	easily	20	carrier
21	journeying	22	playful
23	busiest	24	employment
25	awkward	26	boundary
27	definite	28	encourage
29	harass	30	interrupt

Focus test 12: Sentences 3

1	active	2	passive
3	active	4	passive
5	passive	6	active

7 Mum said that it was time for tea.
8 Joe asked when the holidays started.
9 Jacob queried whether he had to clean out his rabbit.
10 Mia said she was now off to the park.
11 Tom stated that he thought the phone was ringing.
12 I don't want any sympathy.
13 Please can I not have any cheese in my sandwich.
14 I can't find any biscuits!
15 Anika won't catch the bus home.
16 There isn't any fruit growing on the trees.
17 dog's lead
18 Callum's coat
19 teacher's pen
20 policeman's hat
21 painter's radio
22 girl's cake
23–30 "**A**re you awake?" **T**oby whispered. "It is time for our midnight feast**.**"

Focus test 13: Grammar 3

1–6

	Comparative adjectives	Superlative adjectives
Tall	taller	tallest
Tired	more tired	most tired
Good	better	best
Attractive	more attractive	most attractive

7 preposition
8 proper noun
9 common noun
10 connective
11 adverb
12 collective noun
13 pronoun
14 abstract noun
15 verb
16 adjective
17–18 Nina swam in the <u>pool</u>.
    subject pronoun: She
19–20 The children watched the <u>match</u>.
    subject pronoun: They
21–22 The old woman stroked the <u>dog</u>.
    subject pronoun: She
23–24 Tim couldn't wait to go to <u>school</u>.
    subject pronoun: He
25–26 *sprint, saunter*
27–28 *mine, yours*
29–30 *behind, over*

Focus test 14: Vocabulary 3

1 disappear
2 undo
3 inaccurate
4 irrelevant
5 unfriendly
6 impolite
7–12 *Child's own similes describing given subjects.*
13 Better late than never.
14 A rolling stone gathers no moss.
15 You scratch my back and I'll scratch yours.
16 A penny saved is a penny gained.
17 Two heads are better than one.
18 Barking dogs seldom bite.
19–24 visitor, astronaut, gentry, friend, companion, them
25–30 *Child's own answer, for example pyjamas, boomerang, pizza, piano, café, spaghetti.*

Focus test 15: Comprehension 3

1 True
2 Ten thousand soldiers walked in the procession that day.
3 There was a soft jingle from the horses' harness and the creaking gun carriages the horses were pulling.
4–6 'All of England was mourning the death of one man.' (line 3)
'all the people of London were out on the streets' (lines 3–4)
'Ten thousand soldiers marched in procession' (line 6)
7 An ensign is a flag.
8 Yes, the Prince of Wales rode just in front of the funeral carriage.
9 The funeral was held in St Paul's Cathedral, London.
10 *Victory* is the name of Admiral Nelson's ship.
11 This recount is written from Sam's perspective. He was a crew member on HMS *Victory* under Admiral Nelson.
12–13 *Child's own description of Will Wilmet, for example he was the bosun, upset at funeral, kind, thoughtful man.*
14–15 *Child's own interpretation of the feelings on the street on that important day in history.*

Mixed paper 1

1 The Somerton Strawberry Fair has been running for 25 years.
2 The Strawberry Fair is held on the Village Green.
3–4 The Strawberry Fair is held at a time when strawberries are ripe and easily available but also when the weather is likely to be good.
5–6 1 – the local community wait at the tables
2 – tickets are available at the local Post Office
7 'THE WORKS' could include everything – strawberries, cream, ice cream and shortbread.
8–9 *Child's own answer, for example plants and books.*

A4

10 *Child's own thoughts on who will enjoy the evening entertainment – taking into consideration the type of music playing.*

11–12 *Child's own thoughts on whether the evening entertainment is good value for money – taking into consideration that food and a drink are also provided.*

13–14 The poster makes reference to the Saxon church and the ancient lime trees.

15–16 *In the answer, the child needs to recognise that the weather at the weekend could dictate numbers attending. For example if wet, fewer people would attend and therefore income would be lower, and strawberries might be left over.*

17–18 *Child's ideas might include serving the strawberries under cover, for example in the church or under gazebos, selling off strawberries in punnets, moving Barry's Big Band to a different venue, for example village hall.*

19–20 *Child's own ideas on how the poster could be improved, for example more pictures, fewer words.*

21 solidify
22 apologise
23 lighten
24 fossilise
25 intensify
26 ✓
27 ✗
28 ✓
29 ✓
30 ✗
31 unnecessary
32 occurrence
33 suddenly
34 innocent
35 occupation
36–37 *table, chair*
38–39 *love, hate*
40–41 *London, Tom*
42–43 *litter, pack*
44–45 Aimee loved acting in the <u>school play</u>.
subject pronoun: She
46–47 Terry mended his broken <u>bike</u>.
subject pronoun: He

48 Ben ate ravenously *because* he hadn't eaten all morning.
49 The boat broke *as* it crashed against the rocks.
50 Ravi slipped off the pony *although* he had done exactly as he was told.
51 as blind as *a bat*
52 as brave as *a lion*
53 as fresh as *a daisy*
54 as hot as *a chilli*
55 as quiet as *a mouse*
56–60 *enjoyable, excellent, great, skilled, kind, etc.*
61 entertain
62 scare
63 thunder
64 press
65 collect
66–70 *A clause and conjunction added to the given main clauses. A clause is a section of a sentence with a verb.*
71 was
72 Were
73 were
74 was
75 were
76 Can we have tomato ketchup, mushy peas, onion rings and chips with our fish?
77–78 We ran, puffing and panting, trying to catch up with our escaped dog.
79 With a huge shove, the old door finally opened.
80 Hannah was sad as her belongings, her bed and her bike were packed into the removal van.

Mixed paper 2

1 The boys met in the early evening when it was just dark but not too late, as it hadn't got too cold.
2–3 The line 'That smell of burnt leaves, the early dark' suggests that it is autumn. Lines referring to the apples could also be quoted.
4–5 Three boys met in the park.
6 'The trees' green domes' are the leaf canopies of the trees.

A5

ANSWERS

Bond UP TO SPEED English Tests and Papers 10–11+ years

7 The clusters are apples on the lower boughs.

8–9 *Child's answer describing how the boys felt, for example nervous, excited.*

10 The apples were described as 'tasty loot' because they tasted good but were stolen.

11–12 The poet is referring to the whole adventure and the smell of the apples.

13 The poem implies that John is dead, buried under apple trees.

14 The poem is written approximately 40 years after the event as the boys were young when they stole the apples and reference is made to one boy now being 50 years old.

15–16 It is significant that John lies under apple trees after the adventure the boys had, but because it is a French orchard it implies he was killed in the war and buried abroad.

17–18 For example: 'Street lamps spilled pools of liquid gold;' (line 3)
'The breeze was spiced with garden fires.' (line 4)

19–20 *Child's own appraisal of the poem giving reasons for their thoughts.*

21 she's
22 could've
23 it'll
24 wasn't
25 they're
26 *bicycle*
27 *unclear*
28 *telephone*
29 *autograph*
30 *television*
31 elephants
32 dishes
33 wolves
34 zoos
35 lilies
36 The keys were knocked <u>underneath</u> the sofa.
37 The smoke could be seen <u>on</u> the horizon.
38 Jane looked <u>through</u> the keyhole.
39 Dan became caught <u>behind</u> the wheelie bin!

40 The dog slipped <u>off</u> the rock face.
41–42 *old, rickety* gate
43–44 *gleaming, crystal* vase
45–46 *rusty, muddy* bike
47 Robert and Sammy <u>is</u> going on holiday. are/were
48 Laughing <u>were</u> all they could do! is/was
49 Keita the dog <u>were</u> excited about her walk. is/was
50 Jacob <u>are</u> doing homework.   is/was
51 raspberry
52 rattle
53 raven
54 ravioli
55 razor
56 *bright*
57 *young*
58 *pull*
59 *disprove*
60 *robust*
61 *uncaring, thoughtless*
62 *a plant that grows in the sea*
63 *a section of something*
64 *a large number of fish*
65 *a short phrase often used in advertising*
66 statement
67 command
68 question
69 command
70–76 **N**iall peered over the railings. **"L**ook! **I** can see the sleeping tiger.**"**
77 active
78 active
79 passive
80 active

Mixed paper 3

1 Yes, a few spiders are capable of killing humans.

2 Spiders' venom is usually harmless to humans because it is designed to work on the animals that spiders prey on, not humans.

3 No, a Tarantula isn't deadly though its bite would really hurt!

A6

4 If a Brown Recluse spider bites you, the flesh around the bite rots and dies.

5–6 An antivenin is a medicine that works against the venom of specific spiders. It means that, should someone be bitten by a dangerous spider, they have an increased chance of surviving.

7–8 Spiders are more likely to bite when they feel trapped or surprised, e.g. when a spider is resting in gloves and they are then put on.

9 Spiders would have been encountered more often because our primate ancestors used to live where spiders lived, on forest floors or up in trees.

10–11 *It is believed that our fear of spiders is partly inborn and comes from a time when even a bite that was harmless could stop our ancestors from hunting and finding the food they desperately needed.*

12 Most venomous spiders live in jungles and forests.

13 Yes, some spiders eat birds or small mammals.

14 Spiders remove flies, mosquitos and other bothersome insects.

15–16 *Child's own comment on whether we still need to fear spiders and an explanation for their answer.*

17–18 *Child's own comment on what they have learned in this passage and whether it has changed their perception of spiders.*

19–20 *Child's own two questions they would like answered about spiders.*

21 pier
22 conceit
23 neither
24 friend
25 review
26–27 *unfold, undo*
28–29 *disappear, distrust*
30–31 *microphone, microscope*
32 tomorrow
33 wardrobe
34 rhythm
35 succeed
36–39 *Child's own two sentences, each including a preposition and conjunction.*

40–44

	Comparative adjectives	Superlative adjectives
wise	wiser	wisest
angry	angrier	angriest
thoughtful	more thoughtful	most thoughtful

45–46 *sleep, swim*
47–48 *yours, his*
49–50 *slowly, soon*
51 Mister/Master
52 British Broadcasting Company
53 Great Britain
54 anonymous
55 adjective
56–60 iPod, euro, air guitar, computer, email
61 The first in line will be seen to first.
62 A friend that needs your help is a really good friend.
63 It is better to arrive late (or do something late) than not at all.
64 No matter what the situation, however bad, you can always find something good in it.
65 If you are careful with your money, you will be able to save.
66–69 *Two sentences, each with two commas correctly placed.*
70 the man's shoes
71 the child's marbles
72 the bridesmaid's flowers
73 the gardener's spade
74 Leah's earrings
75 Alice's book
76 Helen said she wished she could watch the end of the film.
77 Fred asked if they could dance.
78 Tom screamed that the zombies were coming!
79 Dad said that he thought there was an accident ahead.
80 Kate moaned that the park was closed.

Mixed paper 4

1 Willie needed the lugworms for bait.
2 Willie was first aware of the seals after hearing a strange moaning sound.

ANSWERS

3 The seal pup did not move as it had just been born and was unaware of the dangers of man.

4 Willie planned to take the seal pup home for his bairn/child.

5–6 Willie placed the pup close to the water's edge because he could see the distress of the mother seal.

7 A 'trink' is a stretch where the water flows fast and deep on the high tide.

8 Willie Westness thinks about keeping the pup in a small 'loch' – a Scottish word for lake.

9 Willie had four children nine years later.

10 The children had heard their father say that there were plenty of cockles across the trink.

11 They were probably arguing about whether they should cross the trink because they had been told it was dangerous.

12 Tam was Willie's youngest child.

13 The children didn't notice the tide because they were so busy picking cockles.

14–15 *Child's own description of the two women that appeared.*

16 grey-cloaked; plump; friendly face; round brown eyes

17–18 The message to Willie is saying in return for giving my child back to the sea, I will return your three children to the land.

19–20 *Child's own reaction to the end of the story and whether it surprised them.*

21 comfortable

22 nervous

23 novelist

24 sensible

25 musician

26 class

27 hoof

28 tragedy

29 scissors

30 scratch

31 we + have

32 would + not

33 we + would/we + had

34 it + is

35 she + will

36–41 *Three sentences, each with an adjective and adverb.*

42 pronoun

43 adverb

44 common noun

45 preposition

46 verb/common noun

47 pronoun

48 abstract noun

49 adjective

50 conjunction/connective

51 *airport*

52 *bedtime*

53 *checkout*

54 *downstairs*

55 *eyelid*

56 *fireworks*

57 flee

58 mist

59 plain

60 stares

61 lessen

62–65 *friend, colleague, teacher, companion*

66–80 "Shall we meet at the park after school?" asked Jake.

"Great idea and I'll bring my skateboard," said Mia.

"I'll let the others know," Jake replied, wandering to his lesson.

"Bye," Mia yelled after him.

In each sentence, underline the **object** and write a **pronoun** for each subject.

> Remember: a pronoun is a word usually used to replace a noun.

17–18 Nina swam in the pool.   subject pronoun: _____

19–20 The children watched the match.   subject pronoun: _____

21–22 The old woman stroked the dog.   subject pronoun: _____

23–24 Tim couldn't wait to go to school.   subject pronoun: _____   **8**

Write two examples of each of the following.

> A powerful verb is a verb that adds more interest to your writing.
>
> A possessive pronoun is a pronoun that shows to whom something belongs.
>
> A preposition gives us the position of something in relation to another thing.

25–26 powerful verb   _____   _____

27–28 possessive pronoun   _____   _____

29–30 preposition   _____   _____   **6**

Now go to the Progress Chart to record your score!   Total   **30**

Focus test 14 | Vocabulary 3

Write an **antonym** for each of these words by adding a **prefix**.

> An antonym is a word that has the opposite meaning to another word.

un   im   ir   in   dis

1 appear   _____

2 do   _____

3 accurate   _____

4 relevant   _____

5 friendly   _____

6 polite   _____

6

Write a **simile** using the following subjects.

> A simile is an expression that describes what something is like, for example 'as cold as ice'.

7 sun   _____

8 car   _____

9 beetle   _____

10 diamond _____

11 pillow   _____

12 thunder _____

6

With a line, match the beginning of the **proverb** with its end.

> A proverb is a short saying that gives advice or tells you something.

13	Better late	is a penny gained.
14	A rolling stone	are better than one.
15	You scratch my back	seldom bite.
16	A penny saved	gathers no moss.
17	Two heads	than never.
18	Barking dogs	and I'll scratch yours.

6

Circle any word that applies to both males and females.

19–24

visitor	princess	duke	astronaut
king	gentry	niece	ram
friend	sow	companion	them

6

Write six words that are used in English but originally came from another language.

> Think carefully about the words you choose.
> You could choose words from any country: perhaps from France, India, Australia or Italy.

25–30 _____   _____   _____

_____   _____   _____

6

Now go to the Progress Chart to record your score!   Total   30

Focus test 15 — Comprehension 3

Victory

The sound of the drums was like the beating of a great slow heart. Muffled drums, they were, with black cloth over them. Everything was muffled that day, even the grey, clouded sky. All of England was mourning the death of one man, and all the people of London were out on the streets leading to St Paul's, and all the air was filled with the slow beat of the drums and the unending slow march of thousands of feet. 5

Ten thousand soldiers marched in procession that day, before and behind us, in that long step they keep for funerals, with the hesitation in it that breaks your heart. Marines were marching too, and the cavalry regiments trotting their horses slow, with a soft jingle of harness, and artillery with horses pulling the creaking gun carriages. Every man of us wore black stockings, with black crepe in our hats, and black ribbons hung from the 10 horses' heads. Over the beat of the drums, sometimes you would hear the wailing lament of a pipe band, like London weeping.

And there were we, forty-eight of us from the crew of his flagship HMS *Victory*, walking in pairs: forty-eight seamen and marines, with the senior men up front carrying our poor flag, the tattered white ensign that had flown from the masthead at the Battle of Trafalgar 15 and been shot through and through. The men held it up sometimes to show it to the people lining the streets, and some said you could hear a rustle like the sound of the sea as hundreds and hundreds of men took off their hats in respect. Me, all I could hear was the drums, and the feet, and the boom of the minute guns.

Dozens of carriages creaked along behind us, drawn by more jingling horses, filled 20 with noblemen and officers. Thirty-two admirals in full dress uniform there were at the Admiral's funeral, and a hundred captains. There never was a funeral like it, not even for a king. The Prince of Wales rode in his crested carriage just in front of the funeral car, a long gun carriage made to look like our *Victory*, with high brow and stern, and a canopy swaying above our Admiral's coffin. 25

With music and high words the funeral service lasted for hours, inside St Paul's Cathedral. A great blaze of candles hung from the huge domed roof. At the very end, when the coffin was to be lowered into the ground, we seamen had been told to fold our ensign in ceremony and lay it on the top. But when Will Wilmet, the bosun, and three of the older men took up that shredded white cloth, Will gave a kind of sob – and suddenly all the 30 men were reaching for our sad flag and it came apart, and they stuffed pieces of it into their jackets. And the coffin went down into the crypt, under the stone floor, for ever.

He was a good man, Wilmet. He gave me a scrap of the flag for my own afterwards, outside the cathedral, when we were gathering to march back through the streets of London without our Admiral. 35

"Here, young Sam," he said. "Here's a bit for you. Keep it till you die, and have it buried with you. Your own little bit of Nelson."

From *Victory* by Susan Cooper

Answer the questions.

1 This passage describes a funeral. True or false?

It is true

2 How many soldiers marched in the procession?

There were Ten thousand soldiers

3 What noises does the writer associate with the horses?

Jingiling horses

4–6 Find three pieces of evidence that suggest this was a funeral for an important man.

Three pieces of evidence to suggest it was an important man are 'Ten thousand soldiers marched in procession", "All of England was mourning of the death of one man", "and all the people of London were out on the streets"

7 What is an ensign?

8 Did royalty attend the funeral?

9 Where was the funeral held?

10 How does the title of the story relate to this passage?

11 From whose perspective is this recount written?

12–13 Describe Will Wilmet in your own words.

14–15 Imagine that you were a Londoner on the streets watching the funeral go past. Describe how you and others around you felt.

Now go to the Progress Chart to record your score! Total 15

33

Mixed paper 1

Somerton Strawberry Fair – 25th Anniversary

Date: 7 and 8 July
Time: 10am–5pm
Come and enjoy the STRAWBERRIES!

- Strawberries and cream
- Strawberries and shortbread
- Strawberries and ice cream
- Just strawberries
- or…THE WORKS!

The Village Green becomes transformed as we welcome visitors from far and wide to taste the delights of an English Village Strawberry Fair. Relax under the cooling ancient lime trees while you are waited on by the local community.

Summer Market with stalls selling gifts, clothing, jewellery, honey, food and furniture.

Come and wander through the village's Saxon church where live music will be playing throughout the weekend. The live music includes piano recitals, flute duets, soprano singing. Something for everyone.

On Saturday evening, on the Village Green, we welcome Barry's Big Band. Put on your dancing shoes and for just £5 enjoy the sounds and sights of this top-class band. All the family are welcome, food and a drink provided at no extra cost.

Tickets available from Somerton Post Office or from Somerton Preschool at the village hall.

Answer these questions.

1 How many years has the Somerton Strawberry Fair been running?

_____

2 Where is the Strawberry Fair held in Somerton?

_____

3–4 Give two reasons why you think the Strawberry Fair is held in July.

_____

_____

5–6 Find two pieces of evidence that suggest the locals run the fair.

7 What do you think 'THE WORKS' includes?

8–9 List two other things that could be sold at the Summer Market?

10 Although the poster states that everyone is welcome to the evening entertainment, what groups of people do you think will most enjoy it?

11–12 Do you think that the evening entertainment is good value for money? Why?

13–14 What evidence is there that Somerton is an old, well-established village.

15–16 How could the weather affect the success of the weekend?

17–18 What could the organisers do to overcome the problems of a very wet weekend?

19–20 How could this poster be improved?

_____

_____ **20**

Add the **suffix** _en_, _ify_ or _ise_ to each of these to make a word. Don't forget any necessary spelling changes.

21 solid   _____

22 apology   _____

23 light   _____

24 fossil   _____

25 intense   _____ **5**

Put a tick by the words spelt correctly and put a cross by those spelt incorrectly.

26 natural   ☐

27 oparate   ☐

28 sincere   ☐

29 ridiculous ☐

30 superor   ☐ **5**

Add the correct double letters to complete each word.

    cc   dd   nn

31 u _____ _____ ecessary   32 o _____ _____ urrence

33 su _____ _____ enly   34 i _____ _____ ocent

35 o _____ _____ upation **5**

Write two examples of each of the following.

36–37 common nouns   _____   _____

38–39 abstract nouns   _____   _____

40–41 proper nouns   _____   _____

42–43 collective nouns   _____   _____ **8**

In each sentence, underline the **object** and write a **pronoun** for each **subject**.

44–45 Aimee loved acting in the school play. subject pronoun: _____

46–47 Terry mended his broken bike.   subject pronoun: _____

4

Add a different **conjunction** to each of these sentences.

48 Ben ate ravenously _____ he hadn't eaten all morning.

49 The boat broke _____ it crashed against the rocks.

50 Ravi slipped off the pony _____ he had done exactly as he was told.

3

Finish these **similes**, using your own words.

51 as blind as _____

52 as brave as _____

53 as fresh as _____

54 as hot as _____

55 as quiet as _____

5

Write five **synonyms** for the word 'good'.

56–60 _____   _____   _____

_____   _____

5

Underline the **root words** in each of these words.

61 entertaining   62 scared

63 thunderous   64 pressure

65 recollect

5

37

Add a **clause** with a **conjunction** to each of these main clauses.

66 The thunderstorm was frightening _____

_____

67 Jake fell off the swing _____

_____

68 The children on the rollercoaster screamed _____

_____

69 Dee slipped on the ice _____

_____

70 The teacher spoke quietly to her class _____

_____ **5**

Add 'was' or 'were' in each gap to make the sentences correct.

71 Meg _____ late for school.

72 _____ we on time for the football?

73 The children _____ soaking their dad with a hose.

74 The giant _____ terrifying.

75 Veejay and Tuhil _____ going to the dentist on Monday. **5**

Add the missing commas to these sentences.

76 Can we have tomato ketchup mushy peas onion rings and chips with our fish?

77–78 We ran puffing and panting trying to catch up with our escaped dog.

79 With a huge shove the old door finally opened.

80 Hannah was sad as her belongings her bed and her bike were packed into the removal van. **5**

Now go to the Progress Chart to record your score!   Total **80**

38

Mixed paper 2

The Apple-Raid

Darkness came early, though not yet cold;
Stars were strung on the telegraph wires;
Street lamps spilled pools of liquid gold;
The breeze was spiced with garden fires.

That smell of burnt leaves, the early dark,   5
Can still excite me but not as it did
So long ago when we met in the park –
Myself, John Peters and David Kidd.

We moved out of town to the district where
The lucky and wealthy had their homes   10
With garages, gardens, and apples to spare
Ripely clustered in the trees' green domes.

We chose the place we meant to plunder
And climbed the wall and dropped down to
The secret dark. Apples crunched under   15
Our feet as we moved through the grass and dew.

The clusters on the lower boughs of the tree
Were easy to reach. We stored the fruit
In pockets and jerseys until all three
Boys were heavy with their tasty loot.   20

Safe on the other side of the wall
We moved back to town and munched as we went.
I wonder if David remembers at all
That little adventure, the apples' fresh scent.

Strange to think that he's fifty years old,   25
That tough little boy with scabs on his knees;
Stranger to think that John Peters lies cold
In an orchard in France beneath apple trees.

Vernon Scannell

Answer these questions.

1 At what time of day did the boys meet?

Evening

2–3 In which season is the poem based? Use a line from the poem to support your answer.

In spring 'gorages, gardens and apples to spare' as you get apples grow in spring.

4–5 Where did the boys meet and how many were there?

There were three of them and they met in a park

6 What are 'the trees' green domes' (line 12)?

Green trees

7 Verse 5 mentions the 'clusters'. What are in the clusters?

fruit

8–9 In your own words, describe how the boys felt having climbed the wall into the 'secret dark'.

10 Why were the apples described as the boys' 'tasty loot' (line 20)?

11–12 The poet wonders whether David remembers two things, what two things does he refer to?

13 Why does the poet just wonder what David remembers, rather than David and John?

14 Approximately how many years after the event is this poem written?

15–16 Why is it significant that John Peters lies in a French orchard, beneath apple trees?

40

17–18 What are two metaphors found in this poem?

19–20 How does this poem make you feel? What do you like or dislike about it?

◯ 20

Write the **contraction** for each of these.

21 she + has   = _____

22 could + have = _____

23 it + will   = _____

24 was + not   = _____

25 they + are   = _____

◯ 5

Add a **prefix** to each of these to make a new word.

26 cycle   _____

27 clear   _____

28 phone   _____

29 graph   _____

30 vision   _____

◯ 5

Write the **plural** form of each of these nouns.

31 elephant _____

32 dish   _____

33 wolf   _____

34 zoo   _____

35 lily   _____

◯ 5

41

Underline the **preposition** in each sentence.

36 The keys were knocked underneath the sofa.

37 The smoke could be seen on the horizon.

38 Jane looked through the keyhole.

39 Dan became caught behind the wheelie bin!

40 The dog slipped off the rock face.

○ 5

Write two **adjectives** to describe each of these **nouns**.

41–42 _____, _____ gate

43–44 _____, _____ vase

45–46 _____, _____ bike

○ 6

In each of these sentences a word is incorrect. Underline the word and rewrite it correctly.

47 Robert and Sammy is going on holiday. _____

48 Laughing were all they could do! _____

49 Keita the dog were excited about her walk. _____

50 Jacob are doing homework. _____

○ 4

Put these words in **alphabetical order**.

raven   razor   rattle   raspberry   ravioli

51 _____   **52** _____

53 _____   **54** _____

55 _____

○ 5

Write an **antonym** for each of these words.

56 dull _____

57 elderly _____

58 shove _____

59 prove _____

60 delicate _____

○ 5

42

Write a **definition** for each of these words.

61 selfish

62 seaweed

63 segment

64 shoal

65 slogan

5

What are the following: commands, questions or statements?

66 I would like to make some cakes _____

67 Be quick _____

68 Can you feed the dog _____

69 Stop screaming _____

4

Rewrite this sentence, adding the missing punctuation and capital letters.

70–76 niall peered over the railings look i can see the sleeping tiger

7

State whether each of these sentences has an **active** or **passive verb**.

77 Gina swung on the swing. _____

78 Tim watched the television. _____

79 Ivy was having her hair cut. _____

80 Oscar screamed loudly. _____

4

Now go to the Progress Chart to record your score!   Total   **80**

43

Mixed paper 3

Do we need to be scared by spiders?

There are over 40,000 known species of spider, yet fewer than 30 have
venom that can cause serious illness in humans, and only a few (including
Black and Brown Widow spiders, Funnel-web spiders and Brazilian
Wandering spiders) are capable of killing with a bite. This is because spider
venom typically only works on the animals (usually insects, but sometimes   5
birds and small mammals) that the spider preys on. So most venomous
spider bites cause, at worst, minor illness in humans and other animals not
part of the spider's diet.

In fact, most of the spiders people think are 'deadly' aren't even
dangerous. A bite from a Tarantula, for example, is very painful but   10
certainly won't kill you. A bite from a Brown Recluse spider may look nasty,
as it causes the flesh around it to rot and die, but there hasn't been a single
confirmed death from one of those either.

Even Black Widows, which do have the ability to kill us, hardly ever
succeed in doing so, because they rarely inject more than a tiny amount   15
of venom per bite. Add to that the powerful antivenins (medicines which
work against the venom of specific spiders) that are kept in hospitals to treat
Black Widow bites, and the result is that the death rate has fallen to just one
or two people per year, worldwide.

Most spiders are not aggressive, and prefer not to get close enough to   20
humans to bite them. In fact, most spiders are even less keen on biting than
snakes, and only bite if picked up, prodded or squashed. No venomous
spider will charge or jump at you to bite, like they do in horror movies.
Almost all spider bites happen when people put on gloves, footwear or
other clothing in which the spider was resting. And think about it – if you   25
were stuck in the toe of a giant boot, and a huge fleshy foot came down to
squash you, what would you do? Everything you could to stop it, I should
think. And that's all poor Spidey does.

The lowdown

Spiders, basically, get a bad rap. Our fear of them is deep, because it   30
goes way, way back – perhaps to the time when our primate ancestors
used to sleep on forest floors or up in trees, where they encountered
spiders more often.

At least part of our fear of them seems to be inborn. This is possibly
because that very fear helped our ancestors to survive. While spider bites   35
rarely kill modern humans, it would have been a different story for our
animal ancestors. One painful, swollen bite to the hand or foot could have
stopped them from hunting. That would have made even non-lethal spider
bites deadly in the long run.

44

But when you look at it, we really don't need these fears any more. 40
Hardly any spiders pose a threat to us now, and they're generally easy
enough to avoid, since we no longer have to go rooting around in the
jungles and forests where most of the venomous ones live. If we can tolerate
having spiders around, they actually do us a favour by removing mosquitoes,
flies and other bothersome insects as part of their daily diet. 45

From *Stuff that scares your pants off!* by Glen Murphy

Answer these questions.

1 Are any spiders capable of killing a human?

2 Why is a spider's venom usually harmless to humans?

3 Is a Tarantula deadly?

4 What effect does a bite from a Brown Recluse spider have?

5–6 What are antivenins? What difference have they made?

7–8 When are spiders most likely to bite? Give examples.

9 Why would our primate ancestors have encountered spiders more
often than we do now?

10–11 In your own words, explain where our fear of spiders might come
from.

12 Where do most venomous spiders live?

_____

13 Can some spiders catch birds to eat?

_____

14 How do spiders help us?

_____

15–16 The passage states in line 40 that we no longer need to fear spiders. Do you agree? Why?

_____

_____

_____

17–18 Explain how this passage has changed how you might now react to spiders.

_____

_____

_____

19–20 Write two further questions you would like to ask about spiders that you can't find answers for in this passage.

_____

_____

⬤ 20

Add *ie* or *ei* to each of these to make a word.

21 p ____ ____ r   **22** conc ____ ____ t

23 n ____ ____ ther   **24** fr ____ ____ nd

25 rev ____ ____ w

⬤ 5

Write two words that begin with each of these **prefixes**.

26–27 un   _____   _____

28–29 dis   _____   _____

30–31 micro   _____   _____

⬤ 6

46

Circle the word that is spelt correctly.

32 tommorow   tomorrow

33 wadrobe   wardrobe

34 rhythm   rythum

35 suceed   succeed

4

Write two sentences, each with a **preposition** and a **conjunction**.

36–37 _____

_____

38–39 _____

4

_____

Complete the table.

40–44

	Comparative adjectives	**Superlative adjectives**
wise	wiser	
angry		
thoughtful		

5

Write two examples of each of the following.

45–46 verb   _____   _____

47–48 pronoun   _____   _____

49–50 adverb   _____   _____

6

Write the following **abbreviations** in full.

51 Mr   _____

52 BBC   _____

53 GB   _____

54 anon.   _____

55 adj.   _____

5

47

Circle the words that have come into our language in the last 100 years.

56–60 aeroplane   iPod   euro

         cinema   London   air guitar

         computer   email   car

5

Write the meaning of each of these **proverbs**.

61 First come, first served.

_____

62 A friend in need is a friend indeed.

_____

63 Better late than never.

_____

64 Every cloud has a silver lining.

_____

65 A penny saved is a penny gained.

_____

5

Write two sentences. Each sentence needs to have two commas.

66–67 _____

         _____

68–69 _____

         _____

4

Rewrite each of the following, using only two or three words, one of which should have an apostrophe.

70 shoes belonging to the man   _____

71 marbles belonging to the child   _____

72 flowers belonging to the bridesmaid _____

73 spade belonging to the gardener   _____

74 earrings belonging to Leah   _____

75 book belonging to Alice   _____

6

Write these sentences as reported speech.

76 "I wish I could watch the end of the film," said Helen.

_____

77 "Can we dance?" asked Fred.

_____

78 "The zombies are coming!" screamed Tom.

_____

79 "I think there is an accident ahead," said Dad.

_____

80 "The park is closed," moaned Kate.

_____ 5

Now go to the Progress Chart to record your score! Total 80

Mixed paper 4

One Spared to the Sea

It is many years now since Willie Westness of Over-the-Watter was digging
lugworms for bait in the little sandy bay on the east side of Elsness. By the
time his pail was full, the tide had not yet turned. The trink was still safe to
cross, and he decided to look for driftwood farther along the shore. Then
it was that he heard the cry from the rocks – a moan like that of a woman   5
in pain swelling into a loud, strange sound and dying into a sort of sob. It
seemed to come from the geo, a little inlet hidden behind the rocks and
covered at high tide. Out in the deep water a big seal had raised its head
and was listening and watching intently.

Willie moved quietly towards the geo. Coming around the rocks that had   10
hidden it, he saw, lying on the shelving stone, another big seal. Beside her
was a newborn pup. As the mother began to move, he ran down over the
rocks. The seal flopped into the water, but the pup lay helpless at his feet. It
squirmed as he picked it up, and then pressed against him and nuzzled at
his hand.   15

I'll take it home for the bairn, thought Willie, and keep it in the small loch
at Over-the-Watter.

At the edge of the rocks the mother seal splashed and sobbed in distress.
When he glanced up, she was pulling herself clumsily back out of the water
to lie moaning at the edge, her round eyes full of tears. The pup too gazed   20
at him with soft blurred brown eyes, and nosed at his sleeve. Its little sleek
round head was like a child's …

'Ach, selkie, take thee bairn and be gone wi' ye!' said Willie Westness
aloud. He put the pup down close to the water's edge and watched the
seal come to it. Then he collected his pail of lugworms and trudged back   25
over the trink where the tide was just beginning to run.

Nine years afterwards, Willie Westness had a family of four. One fine day
the three youngest went wading for cockles at the little sandy bay. They
knew well enough that they should not cross the trink, where the water
swept so fast and deep on the high tide. But they had heard their father   30
say that the cockles were better there than in the large bay itself, and after
a little argument among themselves, they crossed over.

"We won't stay long," said Johnny, the eldest.

"We'll hurry back," agreed his sister, Jeanie.

The cockles were plentiful, and they went on gathering. When the pail   35
was nearly full, they turned towards home. The tide was flowing fast. The
trink had widened.

"Hurry!" said Johnny.

But for all that he and Jeanie pulled and scolded, little Tam's fat legs
could not be hurried over the rocks. Every minute the water deepened.   40

The two younger began to cry … but no one appeared across the trink to help them and the water rose steadily.

Then they heard a soft voice singing almost beside them. Two people had come up behind them – two grey-cloaked women that they did not know.

"Come away, bairns," said the elder. She had a plump, friendly face and round brown eyes. "Come away. It will soon be too late." 45

She took little Tam and Jeanie by the hands and led them straight into the water that was now up to their knees where they stood. Up to their middles it rose, and before they had crossed the trink, up to their necks. But held in her firm, warm grasp they kept their footing and found 50 themselves in safety on the far side. Looking back, they saw their brother coming hand-in-hand with the smaller, slimmer woman.

"All's well," said the older woman cheerfully.

"Now take thee father a word from me," said the elder. "Remember now, to say to thee father, Willie Westness, to mind a day when he digged 55 lugworm at the geo, nine summers gone. And say to him that one spared to the sea is three spared to the land."

And she gave them a little push. Obediently they ran. And when they looked back no grey-cloaked women were in sight, and two seals were swimming towards the point of Elsness. 60

Nancy and W. Towrie Cutt

Answer these questions.

1 Why was Willie digging for lugworms?

_____

2 What alerted Willie to the seals?

_____

3 Why did the seal pup not move when Willie ran up to it?

_____

4 What did Willie plan to do with the seal?

_____

5–6 What did Willie do with the pup and why?

_____

_____

7 In your own words describe a 'trink' (line 3).

_____

51

8 This story is based in Scotland. Find a word after the second paragraph that supports this statement.

_____

9 Nine years later, how many children did Willie have?

_____

10 Why did the children want to cross the trink?

_____

11 What do you think the children were arguing about in line 32?

_____

12 What was the name of Willie's youngest child?

_____

13 Why did the children not notice the tide coming in until it was too late?

_____

14–15 In your own words, describe the women that appeared.

_____

_____

_____

16 What adjectives were used to describe the women that could also be used to describe the seals? List your answers.

_____

17–18 What did the message sent to Willie by the elder woman mean?

_____

_____

19–20 Were you surprised by the ending of the story? How did it make you feel?

_____

_____

_____

20

Add the **suffix** to each of these words. Don't forget any spelling changes.

21 comfort + able = _____

22 nerve + ous = _____

23 novel + ist = _____

24 sense + ible = _____

25 music + ian = _____ **5**

Write the **singular** form of each word. Watch out, there is a trick question!

26 classes _____

27 hooves _____

28 tragedies _____

29 scissors _____

30 scratches _____ **5**

Write the two words each **contraction** stands for.

31 we've = _____ + _____

32 wouldn't = _____ + _____

33 we'd = _____ + _____

34 it's = _____ + _____

35 she'll = _____ + _____ **5**

Write three sentences, each including an **adjective** and an **adverb**.

36–37 _____

_____

38–39 _____

_____

40–41 _____

_____ **6**

What parts of speech are each of these words?

42 they   _____

43 silently   _____

44 camel   _____

45 into   _____

46 play   _____

47 we   _____

48 failure   _____

49 rare   _____

50 because   _____   **9**

Add to each of these words to make a **compound word**.

51 air   _____

52 bed   _____

53 check   _____

54 down   _____

55 eye   _____

56 fire   _____   **6**

Write a **homophone** for each of these words.

57 flea   _____

58 missed   _____

59 plane   _____

60 stairs   _____

61 lesson   _____   **5**

Write four words that apply to both males and females.

62–65   _____   _____

        _____   _____   **4**

Punctuate this passage correctly. Remember to start a new line when it is needed.

66–80 Shall we meet at the park after school asked Jake Great idea and I'll bring my skateboard said Mia I'll let the others know Jake replied wandering to his lesson Bye Mia yelled after him

15

Now go to the Progress Chart to record your score!   Total   80